Five Keys to Successful Nonfiction Writing:

How I Write One Book per Month

Matthew Robert Payne

This book is copyrighted by Matthew Robert Payne. Copyright © 2018. All rights reserved.

Any part of this book can be photocopied, stored, or shared with anyone for the purposes of encouraging people. You are free to quote this book, use whole chapters of this book on blog posts, or use this book for any reason if it is to spread the message of Jesus with this world. No consent from the author is required of you.

Please visit http://personal-prophecy-today.com to sow into Matthew's writing ministry, to request a personal prophecy or life coaching, or to contact him.

Cover designed by akira007 at fiverr.com

Edited by Lisa Thompson at www.writebylisa.com You can email Lisa at writebylisa@gmail.com for your editing needs.

The opinions expressed by the author are not necessarily those of Christian Book Publishing USA.

Published by Christian Book Publishing USA.

Christian Book Publishing USA is committed to excellence in the publishing industry. Book design Copyright © 2018 by Christian Book Publishing USA. All rights reserved.

Paperback: 978-1-68411-564-8

Hardcover: 978-1-68411-565-5

Dedication

I am dedicating this book to my high school English teacher, Mr. Harris, who encouraged me to continue writing. He said that although I was not very good with spelling and grammar, I was one of the very best writers that he had ever encountered. He told me that I had a real gift for putting words on a page. This is my forty-first book so far, and without his encouragement to me that day, I am not sure if I would have ever started to write. His kindness continues to inspire me.

Acknowledgments

I want to thank the entire team of people who help to produce each of my books: Bill, my publisher; Lisa, my copy editor; Nicola, my proofreader; and Akirra007, my cover designer. I sincerely appreciate your help with every project.

I want to thank my mother and father for being my parents and for loving me throughout my life. They are so precious to me.

I want to thank all the readers of this book. You inspire me to write.

I want to give my heartfelt thanks to those that have given money to my ministry of producing books. Last but not least, I want to thank my friends who love me: Lisa, Nicola, Mary, David, Michael, and Wendy.

Table of Contents

Dedication 3
Acknowledgments 4
A Note from My Editor 8
Introduction 9
Key 1: First Things First 10
    A. Why You Are Writing 10
    B. Your Audience 10
    C. Your Goals 11
    D. Your Mission 12
Key 2: Book Structure 14
    A. Choosing Your Title 14
    B. Organizing Chapters 15
    C. Deciding on Content 16
Key 3: Writing the Book 18
    A. My Time-Tested Methods 18
    B. Consistent Chapter Lengths 18
    C. Eliminating Fluff and Overwriting 19
    D. Setting Reasonable Writing Goals 20
Key 4: Winning Elements of a Book 22
    A. A Compelling Title that Attracts Readers 22
    B. A Professionally Designed Cover 22
    C. Effective Back Cover Copy 23
    D. Positive Amazon Reviews 23
    E. An Informative Author Page 24
    F. Professional Editing 25
Key 5: Marketing Yourself and Your Book 27
    A. Increasing Social Media Presence 27
    B. Maintaining a Blog, Guest Blogging, and Online Magazines 28

- C. Developing Your Identity as a Writer 29
- D. Understanding the Kindle Select Program 29
- E. Using Other Forms of Marketing 30

How to Write a Nonfiction Book in One Month 32
- A. Selecting a Working Title 32
- B. Writing Chapter Headings 32
- C. Writing Bullet Points 33
- D. Recording the Chapters in Ten-Minute Files 33
- E. Time Frame—Two Days 34

The Manuscript 36
- A. The First Edit of Your Manuscript—Time Frame of Two Days 36
- B. The Second Edit of Your Manuscript 37
- C. Sending Your Book to the Editor 37
- D. Finalizing the Title 38
- E. Ordering the Cover for the Kindle Book 38

Editing 40
- A. Reading Through the Book with Your Editor 40
- B. Waiting for the Third Edit 41
- C. Scheduling Proofreading 41

Publishing Your Book 44
- A. Sending Files to Publisher—Time Frame of One Week 44
- B. Ordering Your Paperback 44
- C. Paperback Published in One Week 45

Important Points 47
- A. Know your subject thoroughly so that you don't have to research it. 47
- B. Have the mental capacity to record for three or four hours in two days ... 48
- C. Develop a great relationship with your contractors: your editor, proofreader, designer, and publisher. 48
- D. Work on different stages of several books at the same time, such as self-editing, Kindle cover design, book recording, and more. 49

Resources 51

A.	My Publisher: Bill Vincent of Revival Waves of Glory Books & Publishing	51
B.	My editor: Lisa Thompson	52
C.	My proofreader: Nicola	52
D.	My graphic designer: Akira007 on Fiverr.com	53
E.	Create Space	53

Closing Thoughts **54**

I'd love to hear from you **57**

How to Sponsor a Book Project **58**

Other Books by Matthew Robert Payne **59**

About Matthew Robert Payne **62**

A Note from My Editor

With the increased availability of self-publishing, nearly anyone can—and even should!—write a book if they have something they want to share with the world. But the process can confuse people who aren't sure how to proceed.

As a prolific writer, Matthew has taken his wealth of experience and compiled his thoughts into an informative book for the reader who is new to book writing and publishing. His insights will help you as you navigate your writing journey.

Matthew addresses numerous questions, such as recording the book, finding professionals to help you with publishing, and other related topics. Best of all, these are practical tips that you can use today in your writing journey. While editing, I even learned a few publishing tips that I will keep at the ready for future reference.

Matthew generously shares his knowledge with you, the reader. I appreciate his kind recommendation of my services and am happy to work with any of you who might need editing help. See my website here or reach me via email at writebylisa@gmail.com.

Blessings in your writing journey!

Lisa

Introduction

Over twenty-five years ago, I was watching a program on television that briefly mentioned a famous writer of fiction. As I recall, the show spoke about how this famous writer produced his books. I was surprised to hear that he used a Dictaphone to record each and every book. He then handed the tapes to his wife, who took it from there and produced his books. I was interested in writing, and at that stage, I had already written a novel. I determined right then and there that if I was ever going to be a serious writer, I too would dictate my books.

Today, that is how I produce the majority of my books, and the process is very easy and fast. The first half of this book can also apply to people who plan to type a book, but my process of how I write a book every month is more suited to people that will dictate their books.

I choose to use a typist. But I have a friend who is a very successful self-published author, and he uses Dragon Dictate, a computer program that writes your spoken words, to produce his books. Of course, Dragon doesn't get every word right, but I have heard that it is easy to use.

If you are serious about producing books, I hope this small book will encourage you to follow my process and even use the people that help produce my books.

Enjoy!

Matthew Robert Payne

April 2018

Key 1: First Things First

A. Why You Are Writing

You have to decide why you're writing. You might write for one or more of the following reasons:
- You have an urge to write and share your life with people.
- You want to write about a topic that is important to you.
- You feel called to write; you feel that writing is in your genes, or it is something that you were born to do. You have a specific message to share with people.
- You have thought of a great and creative idea for a novel that might succeed.
- You want to influence people in government, in society, or in the church.

What is your reason for writing? Writing takes a lot of effort, time, and discipline. When you self-publish, it takes quite a bit of money. So you need to have a solid reason for writing. Writing can be laborious, hard, and a real trial. It can be difficult to write pages, organize a book, edit it professionally, create a striking cover, and publish it. These are all trials in a writer's life. Even when you've written a few books and the process becomes easier, writing is still a trial. So you really have to start with the reason you're writing, which will propel you through the whole writing process.

B. Your Audience

Who are you writing for? Do you have any idea of the type of person who will read your book? For instance, is your book crime fiction, geared for someone who likes crime, murder, or forensic investigations? Who will enjoy your book?

What makes your book stand out? What will make your book memorable for the reader? Do you have a new angle on forensic science? Do you have a unique killer with an unusual psychological profile? Or if you're writing a nonfiction book, what do you want your audience to know? What change do you want to bring about in your audience?

This is a book about writing. As my audience, I want to encourage you to write a book. I want to encourage you to find yourself a professional editor like Lisa, who's edited many of my books. I want you to enjoy the writing process and produce a hallmark in your life, a worthwhile accomplishment, part of your legacy, a great achievement.

Writing is a tremendous activity and an amazing pasttime, but when you produce a book, you need to do so professionally. What do you want to achieve with your audience? Do you want them to be able to professionally produce, write, edit, and publish their own book? Do you want someone who has just been thinking about writing to be a real success when it comes to writing? Do you want to encourage other Christians to live the right kind of life that demonstrates the love of God everywhere they go? You need to think about who your audience is.

C. Your Goals

What are your writing goals? What do you want to achieve? Do you want to write a first novel and then a sequel for many readers, developing a fan base and a following for what you write? Do you want to just write one book because you have a story burning in you that won't go away?

Do you want to write multiple books? Do you want to become an author with a large following of people who read everything that you write? Do you want to just prove a point to your family and show them that you can write? Do you want to prove your worth to someone? Most of all, do you want to prove something to yourself? You might simply have a story in you that you want to write as a novel, a story that won't go away.

Do you want to embark on a writing project to meet a personal goal? Do you want to prove something to other people besides your family? Or do you want to write to instruct people and help them live a better life, encouraging them to take positive steps to improve their lot in life? Do you want to help others improve some aspect of their life by sharing about a subject that you know intimately?

You should have real goals and specific reasons for writing. These goals will help you when you have to spend hours writing your book and when you have to come up with the financial resources to hire a professional editor. When you are going through the process of organizing the publication of your book and you're paying for each aspect of your book production, you will need a concrete reason for making the effort. When you're going through everything needed to add your book to the marketplace, you will need to have real goals and real reasons for writing the book. Those reasons will propel you through the hardships that you might have to endure to release your book into print so that it's available for people to read.

D. Your Mission

What is your mission? I can tell you, as a Christian writer who writes nonfiction books for a Christian audience, my mission is to teach the following:
- How to be loving Christians and how to be the best possible example of Jesus Christ on earth.
- How ordinary Christians can be extraordinary Christians
- How Christians can be an example and a demonstration of love to the community.

I am doing this over the course of time with numerous books.

I want to teach Christians how to not be judgmental or forceful. I want to teach them how to forgive, show mercy, be charitable, be loving, and how to have a successful relationship with God in heaven. These are some of my goals, and this is my mission as a

Christian writer: to change people, help them develop, and become the very best Christians that they can be. I have done a lot of this work in my personal life. I'm using multiple books and thousands of dollars to teach people how to live a life like I demonstrate.

So what is your mission? What do you want to achieve with your book? Do you want to just write an enjoyable novel to read for pleasure? Do you want to write a novel with a lot of lessons in it? Do you want to convey a message through a fictional story to change hearts and change belief systems? Do you want to expose some type of social injustice and use fiction to do so?

What is your mission? You need to work out these things. You need to decide why you're writing. You have to spend some time and find out who your audience is. You have to set some goals and have a reason for writing. You need a mission, a reason to do what you do.

So far, I have written forty-one books, and I have had many reports from my readers, expressing their heartfelt thanks for these books. Many confess that they have been challenged and that they have taken positive steps to change how they live and approach life. The reports continue to come in that confirm that my goals and my mission have been accomplished and that I am making a lasting and worthwhile change in the world. I pray that you not only learn how to produce a book but that you might also receive feedback that confirms that you have reached your goals and accomplished your mission.

Key 2: Book Structure

A. Choosing Your Title

There's a vast difference in sales of a book with a great title and a book with a mediocre or average title. I wrote a book called *Kingdom Nuggets* with over sixty lessons to help growing Christians have a great relationship with Jesus. This deep and comprehensive book showed people how to improve their relationship with Jesus. I called the book *Kingdom Nuggets* because each of the lessons was little nuggets of information.

But the book had two serious problems: neither the cover nor the title was effective. The book style was lacking and was not selling as well as it could have been. I decided to update the cover and change the title of the book to *Finding Intimacy with Jesus Made Simple*. Amazingly, book sales doubled.

As my example shows, the title is important. The title attracts people and draws in readers. Another excellent example is the famous book, *How to Win Friends and Influence People*. Everyone wants friends. Everyone wants to be a person of influence. Dale Carnegie answered those questions for many people with his title and sold millions of copies of his classic book.

How to Write a Book in 60 Days might be another great title for a book. A lot of people are time poor and want to find a way to write a book quickly. This book would tell them how to do so.

You will need to spend some time coming up with a strong title. If you belong to a writers' group on Facebook or in person, you could make a list of titles. Other people can vote on the best title, the title that promises the most benefit for the readers. I have a friend who is a successful full-time writer. He writes as many as ten titles, and his wife picks out the title that they decide to use. He comes up with the titles, and the editor side of his wife chooses the one they will use.

You have to remember, especially with nonfiction, that people want something: they want to improve or have a better life. If your book promises them a way to lead a better life or promises some great benefits to them, the reader might click on your book and buy it because it promises something they want.

The title also gives you a guide as to what the book will be about and helps you stay on track while you're writing. The title will guide you all the way through the writing process. For that reason, even if you have not come up with the final title, you have to at least find a working title.

B. Organizing Chapters

Your book has to have some structure to it. Most books produced in the world have different chapters. Chapters allow a person to read a certain amount of your message at one time. Many readers use a chapter break to stop reading for a break. Chapters also allow you to make your point in bite-sized chunks. In e-books, chapters allow the reader to easily navigate through the book.

We have discussed that you need a working title as you write. The same thing applies to chapter titles. You need to deliver the benefits of what your title promises within a certain number of chapters in your book. I suggest that you play some anointed music to inspire you. After that, I sit down with a pad of paper and write the first and fundamental chapter title, the beginning of what my message will be about. I then write a second chapter title that builds on that fundamental foundation, and then a third chapter title that builds on that. I write out the titles of all the chapters in a progressive format so that each chapter title builds on the previous chapter title in a logical order.

Try to plan each chapter so that it has about the same amount of content. For example, most of the chapters might be about five pages long. If another subject will take fifteen pages to describe, split up that subject into three sections with the same chapter title:

part one, part two, and part three of that subject. You can also come up with different names for each chapter if you prefer.

You will want to keep some conformity. As you decide on chapter titles, work out how long it will take to describe or fill out those chapters with the necessary information. The chapters could be anywhere from two to five pages each. Whatever you decide, please keep each chapter uniform in length.

I carry out this process every time I sit down to prepare a book. I write down a working title for the book, which usually becomes the final book title. For example, for this book, as Lisa and I were editing, we decided to add the word nonfiction to the book title. This helps further clarify exactly what the book is about.

After I finalize the book title, I then sit down with a pad of paper and listen to some Christian music. I find inspiration and write out ten to twenty chapter titles or more in a progressive format.

Each chapter's subject matter builds on the previous chapter so that I end up with compelling points throughout the book and a strong conclusion. I carefully plan the chapter titles to lay the groundwork for a message that can help a person progress and change their thought processes and make decisions as they go through my book. You don't want to write the deep and complex part of your argument at the very beginning of the book. You want your readers to progress from simple thoughts to more complex ideas toward the end of the book.

C. Deciding on Content.

When you've written out your chapter titles, you can follow a similar pattern to the one used in this book. The title of this chapter was "Book Structure." Then I used the following three sub-headings: "Choosing Your Title," "Organizing Chapters," and "Deciding on Content." This helped me establish structure for what to say in each chapter.

Once you've written your chapter titles, you can write out some bullet points, including points and even hints to some of the stories and illustrations that you will use as you progress through each chapter. As you record each bullet point, you are expanding on the information in the chapter. This will help you develop an outline as you finalize your content for each chapter.

Flesh out each chapter, giving it structure and drafting bullet points of what you want to say. But you don't have to flesh out the whole structure of the entire book at once. You can take your time or work on a chapter every day until you finish. You might not know exactly what you will say in chapter two until you've written chapter one.

You might choose a different approach and not flesh out the structure until you've written the previous chapter. Even so, you should write down the chapter title and have a general idea of what you will say. Then write bullet points and possible arguments on a pad of paper that you plan to make in the chapter that you will write. That is what I did in this book.

Sometimes, I simply write out chapter headings, and I record voice files and depend on my creativity for what I say. I might not always use bullet points. But when I write a book without dictating it, I often use this process. Some people can take many months to write all the chapter summaries, and they don't even start to write the first chapter until they have done all that preparation. The more time you spend in preparation, the better the result will usually be. Of course, some people might use all the planning to procrastinate when it comes to sitting down and writing the actual book. Don't let that be you.

Key 3: Writing the Book

A. My Time-Tested Methods

You might be really surprised to know that I dictate the majority of my books. I write the title of the book like I've discussed, and then I write down the chapter titles. I then flesh out what I'm going to say in each chapter. I start a recording program on my Apple Mac called QuickTime, and I record a ten-minute file for each chapter. I cover everything I need to say in the chapter in one file, or I make multiple chapter titles for a subject that will be longer than three pages or ten minutes of recording time.

B. Consistent Chapter Lengths

In the process of recording a book, I'm consistent in chapter lengths because I limit myself to ten to twelve minutes per recorded file. As you write a book, try to be consistent in the length of each chapter. You can organize this effectively by thinking about each chapter title. Each chapter title should cover enough material so that each chapter is about the same length.

As I mentioned before, if you have a subject that will take about fifteen pages to cover, you will want to do three, five-page chapters rather than one, fifteen-page chapter. Each chapter can have the same name and be labeled part one, part two, and part three.

Readers can be distracted when the number of pages in a chapter jumps around from seven pages to two pages to five pages and so forth. This seems unprofessional and off-putting. But this doesn't hold true for fiction books as chapter lengths can vary greatly. One of the aims of your book is for the reader not only to buy the book but to finish the book. So in your planning stage, when you're deciding what to say, make sure to plan a consistent amount of material under each chapter title. Again, I will repeat myself here: You want people to finish your book.

As you flesh out your chapters, if you find you have a lot to say in one of the chapters, just write a second chapter and add enough material to make a whole new chapter. As I said before, try to make each chapter a consistent length. You can do that by writing the chapters in Microsoft Word or another word-processing program and making them a similar word count. Or you can record each chapter like I do in ten-minute files.

C. Eliminating Fluff and Overwriting

Some writers tend to think that the length of the book really shows how strong the writer is or how important the subject is. Some books take twice as long to say what could be written in half the length. Some writers like to go on and on and on with what they have to say, and they seem to be padding the word count in the book. They seem to try to aim for a certain number of pages in the book to make it longer. I call that fluff or padding. I think it's really silly and unprofessional to write a book like that.

Be sure to make your point, describe your point, illustrate your point, write your conclusion, and then make your next point. Don't fill your book with extra material or write just for the sake of writing. Be concise, be relevant, and certainly mention all the illustrations that will make your point. But if you have a choice between using two or three illustrations, you might want to choose two illustrations instead of having too much information. As you go through this book, you will find me repeating certain points. The repetition is to help cement the process in your mind, not to just add words.

I have a friend who is writing her first book at the moment. She is struggling with this issue. God spoke to her and told her that she likes the sound of her own voice. We laughed a little about that and then talked seriously. She said that she really has to work on cutting down her word count and only saying what is necessary and not just talking for the sake of giving needless information.

It's very clear in all of my books that I haven't written too much just for the sake of writing or of making the book longer. I've been accused of doing that, but it's certainly not my intention or what I try to do. As a side note, my editor cut more than two thousand words or about 15 percent of this book during the editing process. This eliminates repetitive information and streamlines reading so that the book flows more smoothly.

Don't feel that your book has to be a certain length or think that no one will read your book if it's only forty pages. People will spend ninety-nine cents for a twenty-page Kindle book. So anything over twenty pages is acceptable.

Write as many pages as you need to explain your concept and make your argument. Don't write ten or even five pages more. Be diligent and responsible in your writing, and don't write just for the sake of writing to fill up space. You will not be perceived as more intelligent or more of an authority on a subject if you write more. In fact, people might actually think the opposite—that you're less intelligent if you ramble without making your point.

I've heard a person say, "The meaning of life is finding out why you live and doing that with such excellence that you bring glory to God." As a Christian, I feel that this is the best statement on the meaning of life I've ever heard even though it's just a short statement. You could write a whole book about the meaning of life or just sum up what you want to say with that quote. I personally think that the quote is better than any book that could be written about it. Please don't feel that you have to fill up hundreds of pages for your book to be noticed.

D. Setting Reasonable Writing Goals

If you are writing and you have a full-time job, you might be time poor. Many books on writing will suggest that you write something every day. I'm not a believer in that, but that method works for some people.

I would rather encourage you to be conscientious and true to yourself when it comes to writing. Don't sit down and write when you're not in the mood. You can try that, but I find that if I try to dictate a book or write a book when I'm not in the mood, it's not inspired. I have done it before, and it simply does not work for me.

Be responsible to set time aside so that you have a set writing schedule. Be careful to arrange the time so that you can complete your book within a certain amount of time. But certainly, don't be too hard on yourself when it comes to writing your book. Write when you have the time and when you feel inspired. Don't put pressure on yourself to achieve a certain amount of words every day or every week when you could produce better material if you were inspired or in the mood with time to write.

Key 4: Winning Elements of a Book

A. A Compelling Title that Attracts Readers

As we discussed in Key 2, you need to find a great title. Spend some time and even seek other people's advice on a title. Don't be too quick to just choose one right title and accept that title but go through a process of writing numerous titles and asking for people's advice and requesting votes for the best title.

I'm part of a writers' group on Facebook, and you can join that writing group by clicking the link here.

You can post your book titles in the group, and the members will help you vote for the best title. It's a Christian writers' group, but we're open to writers of any belief, and certainly, you could join the group just to find out more. It's very helpful to belong to a writers' group.

B. A Professionally Designed Cover

Some terrible covers from self-published books sadly exist on Amazon. So many people go to the effort and write a great book, spend time and money having the book professionally edited, work really hard to produce strong content, but fail to have a cover designed by a professional graphic designer. This is a grave mistake. Your book sales will dramatically improve with an attractive cover.

I gave the example of a previous book, *Kingdom Nuggets*, with an ordinary title that didn't promise any benefit. I changed the title to *Finding Intimacy with Jesus Made Simple*, and then the book sold a whole lot better. The second part of that story was that I also changed the cover and made sure it was more attractive.

I totally redid the book. The content inside remained the same, but the cover of the book and the new title just made the number of book downloads increase dramatically. Please don't go through the process of writing a book, having it edited, and then not having an attractive and professionally designed cover. Don't make that mistake. It's a total waste of your time as a writer.

C. Effective Back Cover Copy

You want the text from the back cover of your book to promise a very real benefit to the reader. Allow the back-cover text to further tell how the reader will be better off and in a better place if they read your book.

Sometimes, as the writer, you can be close to your book and so personally involved with it that you don't have an objective view of what your book is actually about and the benefits of your book. For this reason, you might need to hire a writer or a professional editor to read your book and write the back-cover description for your book.

I've written so many books now that I find that I can sit down and write engaging copy for the back cover of my books. I have a professional editor in Lisa who helps me touch up and edit what I say so that it sounds clearer and more beneficial to attract readers to the book.

With your first book, you will probably need some help with this part of your book. Consider submitting your proposed back-cover description to your writers' group for other members to give you their tips and advice on proper wording.

D. Positive Amazon Reviews

At the end of your book, include an appeal for people who have enjoyed your book to do you a favor and write a positive review of it. You can sadly find books on Amazon with nice covers and interesting titles but no reviews on the Amazon sales page.

I am time poor and only invest time in reading books with solid reviews that seem attractive to me. I have been spoiled by Amazon. I just won't trust a book based on its title and back cover unless I can read a number of positive reviews. Reviews are very hard to get. It's hard to have your friends read your book and write a positive review for you. It's also illegal to pay people to write reviews. But you can give people a free book if they promise to review your book. Even so, they might not follow through, so it is difficult to get positive reviews.

Like I have shared, one of the best ways that I get positive book reviews is to write a paragraph or two in the back of each of my books, encouraging the readers to post a review. I saw another popular writer, Adam Houge, appeal to readers to write a book review. If you check out his books on Amazon, you will see that each of his books has plenty of reviews.

Not everyone who reads my books writes a review, but I know other writers that don't invite people to write a review, and they lack reviews for their books.

Unfortunately, the success of your book can depend on positive reviews. If you have had a book on Amazon for six months with no positive reviews, it certainly won't attract as many downloads as a book that has even four or five kind reviews.

E. An Informative Author Page

Another simple feature that doesn't cost you a lot of time is to make sure you go to Amazon Author Central and produce your own author page. This is a link that's on the product page that gives more information about the author. It allows you to write a biography of yourself with a page where all your books can be found and displayed.

This is important even if you just have one book because you have the chance to write something that tells the reader a little bit about yourself that's not on the back cover of your book. I utilize my author page well. I've edited my biography there about ten times. I keep on refining it and making it more attractive and more appealing. You can also share your email address and your website or blog address on the author page. The author page will display your blog posts and take people to your blog. Therefore, people who are thinking of buying one of your books can research you, and you have a better chance of converting their efforts into a sale.

F. Professional Editing

A book needs to be professionally edited by a qualified editor to be a true and lasting success. So many self-published writers don't spend the money needed to hire a professional editor. This can be a disastrous mistake for a writer.

When someone takes the time to write a harsh review on Amazon about your book's poor editing, it is too late to edit your book.

I have been writing for a number of years, and I have read quite a number of books by self-published writers. I can handle a few typos and mistakes, but some people cannot read poor quality books. I know writers who have published multiple books and who want to eventually make a living from writing that do not hire professional editors. In my opinion, this is a grave mistake.

Do not hire your mother or other relative who took English classes twenty years ago in college. Do not hire some random person who says they will edit for free. Take the time to research a potential editor and only hire a truly qualified person.

For many years, I used someone from the Philippines to edit my books. I found her on a freelance website. But my books contained numerous mistakes. Since I began using Lisa, I no longer have those issues with my books.

It is better for you to save up for six months to pay for a professional editor than to publish a book without professional editing.

Key 5: Marketing Yourself and Your Book

A. Increasing Social Media Presence

As a writer, you need to have readers. There seems to be little point in writing a book with only two downloads each month. And believe me, I have books that only fifteen or twenty people downloaded in a month because the books weren't attractive. If that were the best book that I had produced, I'd be very sad.

Some people feel that they will write a best-selling book just because they've come up with a great idea, a new title, an attractive cover, solid editing, and a well-packaged book. But if nobody knows about you, how will they find you and buy your book?

Of course, Amazon searches help people find your book. But for an effective search, you need the following:
- Strong keywords
- An engaging title
- The ability to rank in an Amazon search. This means that you show up on the first page, not the twentieth page when someone searches your key words.

Without these items, your book won't do well. If you're on the twentieth page, no one will ever find your book and download it. To avoid this, you need to invest your time on social media and get a following of friends and people that know you as part of your tribe, those that follow and love you who will help buy and promote your books.

Even successful preachers and pastors who produced a book sometimes have lackluster sales simply because they haven't put a lot of time into increasing their presence on social media and increasing ways to market their book. If you just post once a week on Facebook or on social media, you might want to take a year to build a profile for yourself with a solid following before you produce your book.

B. Maintaining a Blog, Guest Blogging, and Online Magazines

Another professional marketing tool and way to build an audience and build an email list is to run a blog. I still don't have a professional email list, but tutorials, videos, and books can teach you how to build an email list so that you can email all your readers and blog followers every time you post a blog.

Maintaining a blog is very helpful, and on your Amazon Author Page, you can include a link to your blog. Readers can then find your books on Amazon and go and read your blog posts. They will see that you're a strong writer and start to follow you.

Another way you can promote yourself is to do guest blogging and network with other writers and those with similar followings and ideas as you. You can ask if you can do a guest blog post on their blog. In this way, their readers and followers can read what you write and possibly subscribe to your blog and follow you if they like what you say.

When an authority has a guest on their blog, the blogger's followers usually respond well. It carries authority with their friends and can help promote you. You can do the same on your blog and invite other strong writers to do guest blog posts on your blog. You can increase your readership and increase the authority of your voice to people.

You can also market your books or your own name through various online magazines and websites. For example, a Christian organization, Identity Network, sends out daily emails of their online magazine. I've contributed four or five times to them, which increases my visibility among Christians so that my name is out there. Readers from Identity Network then go to my website for prophecy requests, and I give personal prophesies for people. This is another way to attract attention to your books and to your website.

C. Developing Your Identity as a Writer

It might take a while for you to develop your identity as a writer. It might take a number of books or several years of blogging. When I had written about twenty books and had been blogging for a while, I started to feel that I was an established writer. Now I consider myself a writer and identify as a writer.

You carry authority and confidence when you identify as a writer. This includes introducing yourself as a writer to people wherever you go: on public transport, to random strangers, and to people at church. This also encourages people to follow you. When you feel that you're just a person who has written a couple of books, but you don't identify as a writer, you come across with less confidence and authority. This translates into fewer followers and less confidence in you.

When you identify as a writer with the confidence of a writer, and you know that that's your life's calling, that translates into higher book sales.

D. Understanding the Kindle Select Program

Amazon has a program called the Kindle Select Program that allows you to make your books exclusive to Kindle and to promote your books for free for five days every ninety days. You can make your book free on Amazon at least one day each month, which will attract quite a few readers.

Many times, I have more downloads of my book in one day when I have it free than I do for a whole month of paid downloads. In this way, Kindle Select helps you get your name out. When you have forty books like I do, promoting one book for free can attract a lot of readers who read that book. They find out that you have forty books, which produces a new reader who follows you as a favorite author. Enrolling your book in the Kindle Select Program is a very wise idea and not being enrolled can hurt book sales. To be enrolled in the Kindle Select Program, your book can only be sold on Amazon and cannot be available on any other platform. This doesn't matter as Amazon accounts for more than 90 percent of e-book sales.

When you include your book in the Kindle Select Program, readers can also enroll in Kindle Unlimited and Kindle Prime. They can pay a certain amount per month to read an unlimited number of books on Kindle. When you belong to the Kindle Select Program, they can read your book for free through Kindle Unlimited. Every time someone reads your book for free, Kindle pays you a certain fee.

You aren't short changed by Amazon if you put your book in Kindle Unlimited, but once again, it allows people to sample your book for free so that they can get to know you as an author. They probably wouldn't have read your books otherwise because they're in Kindle Unlimited for a reason. If you can give someone the opportunity to read your book for free, you can successfully market your own book.

E. Using Other Forms of Marketing

You can advertise on both Amazon and Facebook to promote your books. You can also advertise your book in both paper magazines and online magazines although I've never done this. I focus on writing books and making them as professional as possible.

I have friends who are writers who have used advertising on Facebook and on Amazon. They have books that are priced at $9.99, and so they make enough money to pay for clicks. They advertise a lot, which works for them. My books are ninety-nine cents on Kindle, so I don't have the margin to pay for advertising, but I know it can work for you. Like anything, advertising is a science, and you can have positive or negative results, according to how you apply yourself. Do your research in this area to see what would work best for you.

How to Write a Nonfiction Book in One Month

The Recordings

A. **Selecting a Working Title**

You don't need to have the title of the book finalized when you start to record your book. But it might be smart to have a title that describes what your book will be about before you start. Like I suggested at the beginning of the book, you can spend some time writing out titles and then choosing the best one so that you have a working title for the book.

Come up with a number of working titles and then select one. The title should describe your whole book. You need to have a basic idea of what you're writing about. Selecting a working title is part of how I write one book per month. I will describe more of that process in the following pages.

In the past twelve months, I've written fourteen books, and so I'm qualified to write on this subject. Some people write many books on various fiction or nonfiction subjects, such as how to write a book in sixty days. Yet the quality of their books is lacking if you read more than one of their books. All of my books are great reads that have been edited with excellence. People often express their satisfaction with the quality. Many of my readers start with just one of my books but go on to read more of them.

B. **Writing Chapter Headings**

After you select the working title, you should then write out chapter headings. I put on some music and get into the presence of

God, connecting with the Spirit of God. If you are not a Christian, you won't understand what I'm talking about, but you want to get into a zone where you are inspired. You can then write out consecutive chapter titles as I shared in the past section. You should start with a foundational chapter title and then build on that foundation one after the other. You want to write chapter titles that will have an equal amount of writing in each chapter. I already made that point.

If one subject will take many pages to cover, you want to break up that topic, adding two to three chapter titles to cover that section. List those as part one, part two, part three, and so forth as needed.

C. Writing Bullet Points

Once you have written your chapter titles, you will want to type them up in Microsoft Word and then write out bullet points. With this book, I have a file showing the bullet points that I am using for each section. I keep what I call a run sheet with chapter titles and four or five bullet points per chapter. I just record one audio file that covers all the material under each bullet point before I move on to the next one.

I make ten-minute recordings for each chapter. If you have five bullet points, then you have about two minutes of recording time for each bullet point. This allows you to pace yourself and gives you an idea of the time frame. You might spend three minutes on one bullet point or one minute on the next one. You can flesh out what you plan to say in the chapter. Personally, I like a book with bullet points in it. It seems to break up the reading, just like chapters break up reading.

D. Recording the Chapters in Ten-Minute Files

The place where I have my files typed up allows me to have a twelve-minute file in the recording. Fiverr.com only allows me to make my recordings a maximum of about thirty megabytes or about twelve minutes of recording time. I limit myself to ten-minute recorded files so that the files are small enough to upload.

I have adjusted to that and make sure that each of my chapters is no longer than a ten-minute file. I go from bullet point to bullet point, recording what I have to say. If I end up going longer than ten minutes, I do a second recording and just include that extra five minutes in the next chapter. Chapters might vary slightly in length from five to six pages, but I record each of the chapters in ten-minute recordings.

In this recording session, I'm recording six chapters while sitting down. I'll finish one chapter, save it, record the next chapter, save it, and so on until I finish recording.

E. Time Frame—Two Days

For a medium-sized book of thirty thousand words, I take two days to record about twenty to thirty chapters. I'll sometimes sit down and record the ten-minute files for two or three hours, one after the next. Other times, I record all thirty files in one sitting, which works out to be five hours of recording.

Pick a time when you're feeling energized, when you're feeling that your intuition is working well, and when you're feeling inspired. You can sit down and record all your chapters at once. A typist can later transcribe them. You will need to have some idea of what you're speaking about. You want to make sure that your readers receive a quality product and not just a lot of hot air with useless information.

You can't record a book a month if you don't have the information and the knowledge to share with others. As I said, I produced fourteen books in the last twelve months, which is a lot of information on many subjects. I was able to do a great job of recording, and I produced high quality books. Please note that I am not boasting here. Although this is my opinion, my readers regularly comment on the excellent quality of my books.

With this process, you might take between half an hour to two hours to decide your chapter headings. It might take you a day to select your chapter titles. You should plan this part of your book well as the chapter titles and the subsequent content make up the information in your book and how worthwhile that is to people.

When speaking, you don't need to worry about pauses and *ums* and *ahs* as you record. The typist will remove all of them for you.

The Manuscript

A. The First Edit of Your Manuscript—Time Frame of Two Days

After you record your manuscript with all thirty files, you send them to a typist to be typed up. That can take three or four days, depending on the typist's schedule.

In the meantime, you can work on something else related to your book. I'm always working on a book. Once the typist returns the file, he or she might have misunderstood some words or even completely missed other words. You will need to make corrections to the typing and read through your manuscript and edit it. You can also edit what you said and rewrite sentences to make them sound clearer. You should not rush this part. Take your time and be in an energized and healthy state of mind when you do this.

You might have started sentences with and, so, or but. Eliminate these beginning words to strengthen your writing. As you self-edit, you will want to go through each paragraph of your manuscript line by line, sentence by sentence. Make sure that everything makes sense to you. Of course, everything that you say has to be clear so that when you send your manuscript to your editor, he or she understands what you're saying to properly copy edit your book. If needed, your editor can rewrite what you say.

Self-editing about a hundred pages (thirty thousand words) might take you anywhere from two to seven days. The length of time it takes is not that important. You don't have to follow my directions to the letter. You don't have to write a book in exactly four weeks. You could take six or eight weeks if you are more comfortable writing at a slower pace or if you are just starting out as a writer. Take your time when self-editing your manuscript. If you become tired or if you're not in the mood, don't work on your manuscript. Work on it when you have the time and the mental focus to go through the typed content.

If you come across a sentence that you don't understand because the typist has made an error, either remove the sentence or rewrite it so that you can understand it. Read the sentences before and after the sentence in question to help understand the context.

Make sure each paragraph flows smoothly and that you know what you are saying because you want to make sure that you make sense with coherent thoughts so that your editor can read your book and understand it. You don't want to give your editor a sloppy book that hasn't been self-edited. You want the information to be clear so that you don't waste your editor's time. You don't want your editor to have to guess at the points that you are making.

B. The Second Edit of Your Manuscript

Yesterday, I completed a second edit of a one-hundred-page manuscript (about thirty thousand words) in a day. It took me just a few hours to complete it, and I finished in one session. When you do the second edit, it's almost as if you are just reading a book. You are checking to see that it makes sense and flows well. You might need to delete extra words in some places and add words in other places to clarify your meaning. You might need to remove and, but, and because at the beginning of each sentence. You can keep cleaning up minor mistakes and rewording anything that isn't clear or anything you missed in the first round of edits.

Sometimes during the first editing round, you're focused on how well the book reads, and you forget to pay attention. You read something, and you are distracted and fail to see that it doesn't make sense. When you come back the second time, you catch these mistakes. Use the second edit to make sure that everything reads correctly and that it flows well. By the time you finish the second edit, your manuscript should read smoothly.

C. Sending Your Book to the Editor

You will need to send your editor an email with the file. I have an excellent editor, and we have worked on more than twenty books together. We have a tremendous working relationship. I'm sure she'd love to work with you if you'd like to contact her. I have her contact information later in the book in the resources section. It takes just a few seconds to attach the manuscript file to an email and send it to your editor.

D. Finalizing the Title

You will need to decide on your final title. In order to have a book cover created, you have to choose a title. I said earlier in the book that you could join a writing group on Facebook and give them five or so suggested titles. They can vote on the title that they think is best. They might edit the titles and come up with new ideas. I come up with my best title idea, and then I send it to my editor. She fixes it or edits the title for me. She's very good at helping me with a title. Once you have chosen the title, you can send it to your cover designer.

E. Ordering the Cover for the Kindle Book

Once you have decided on the title, you can order your cover. I go through a paid photo database like Shutterstock and select a picture that I want on the cover. Please don't just pick a random picture off the internet as you might violate copyright laws. Go through a website specifically designed to provide you with photos. I've become quite experienced at picking photographs that will suit the title and the theme of my book to convey the message that I want to communicate. My cover designer is also quite talented at picking out photographs. He sometimes will design a cover from scratch if I don't have a photo. My cover designer includes the purchase of up to three photos in his price. But I usually choose the pictures myself and put in an order for him to create the cover.

Ordering the cover only takes about five minutes, but the cover designer might take up to a week to return the cover to you. While you're waiting for the cover, your editor can be working on the first round of edits.

The length of time the editor takes can vary. Lisa is working with another editor who is booked ten months out, but Lisa is generally booked from a week to three months ahead. A twenty-thousand-word book will also take much less time to edit than a one-hundred-and forty-thousand-word book. Keep in mind that a great job at self-editing will also make your editor's job go much more smoothly and might even cost you a little less.

Editing

A. Reading Through the Book with Your Editor

If your editor can begin working on your book immediately, the first round of copy edits can take anywhere from one to three weeks, depending on the length of the book. Lisa and I have a unique, three-stage process that we use for editing a book. Lisa will copy edit my book and even rewrite my sentences if needed to make the wording clearer. She also handles many behind-the-scenes issues, such as writing back cover copy, verifying all scripture verses, adding hyperlinks, checking for formatting consistency, adding and reviewing footnotes, and more.

I do not enjoy editing, so I don't look at the tracked changes, but she can send you a Microsoft Word file that shows exactly what she changed. I am not interested in that, so she just sends me the corrected version with the changes accepted.

The editor and I then do the read aloud, which means that she copy edits the book and then sends me the manuscript with the changes. She will then call me on the phone, on Skype, or on FB messenger. We actually read through the whole book together and make further edits to bring clarity to the book so that it is as perfect as possible.

The benefit of reading the book out loud is that you can hear how the book will sound to readers, whether they read silently or use a program like Audible. You have added a second sense, hearing, to the first sense of sight to help find additional mistakes and make your book the very best that it can be.

She reads for two hours, so reading the entire book can take from two to ten sessions, depending on the length of the book. One of my books was a hundred thousand words, which took ten reading sessions and twenty hours. But most of my books are shorter and only take three or four sessions or six to eight hours. We can read from eight- to ten-thousand words per session.

You need to be in a positive frame of mind when you read. Don't schedule these sessions if you have a really busy week at work or if you will be overly tired. Consider your work schedule so that you can concentrate on what you are reading.

Lisa and I usually read on consecutive days, but sometimes she needs a day off to rest her voice. So we might read together on Monday and Tuesday and then take a break on Wednesday. We might read again on Thursday and Friday. Whatever you decide, make sure that you can focus and that you are in positive spirits.

Lisa is friendly and easy to work with. If you're under the weather and not feeling your best, you can reschedule the reading. This is one of the most important parts of the editing process and should be given top priority of your time and mental attention. It's imperative that your book reads well. You need to focus and be in a place where you can concentrate on editing your book with Lisa.

B. Waiting for the Third Edit

Once you finish reading the book out loud, Lisa will normally take about a week to do the last round of edits. In that week, she will hyperlink books that you've recommended in your book so that they are active links. The reader can click the link and go straight to Amazon to buy the book. My books have a lot of scripture references, and she checks them all to make sure that they have been perfectly quoted, according to the listed Bible version. She then makes any necessary corrections. She does a final read through of my book during that time so that the book is as clean as possible.

C. Scheduling Proofreading

I have a friend, Nicola, who noticed a few mistakes in some of my books. She said that she'd be quite happy to proofread my books. It's nearly impossible to find every single mistake in a book, even in traditionally published books. Even a knowledgeable editor won't be able to find every single mistake.

When you're reading a book, you read what you think it says and what you want it to say instead of the words that are actually there. You can overlook errors. My proofreader takes the book from Lisa and then thoroughly reviews it. She doesn't change the wording or the content, but she checks for typos, missing letters in words, missed punctuation, spelling mistakes, and any other errors in the manuscript.

Nicola is a personal friend of mine, so we have a great relationship. She normally takes one or two days to proofread the book. She submits any changes to Lisa, who then reviews her suggested changes and makes the necessary corrections. In this way, the manuscript is brought to an even higher standard of perfection.

As a writer, you need an experienced editor and an experienced proofreader. You want to release the best possible product to your readers: quality books with as few mistakes as possible.

As a writer, you will develop a reputation, especially if you plan to release a book a month. You want your readers to be able to read your manuscript with little to no errors in it so that they're not turned off by the mistakes. They might be fascinated with your subject content, but they might not be impressed with the quality of your writing. Lisa is a very knowledgeable editor, and Nicola's an excellent proofreader. They work well together as a team.

Proofreading might take up to two days, so the entire editing process can take up to three weeks. My point here is to write a book each month. I always have two or three projects in process so that delays in editing or in another part of the process don't affect me and upset my schedule. While one book is being edited, I'm working on another book. I am having the files typed up for a second book and proofreading and editing yet a third book. For example, Lisa is editing a book right now. Today I just sent her another book to be edited, and I'm working on this book tonight, recording these files. I also plan to record another book tomorrow night. I am presently working on four books that are all in different stages. Whenever you're working on multiple projects, you can more effectively use your time so that you average a book per month. One month last year, I published three books in three weeks.

I don't want the title of this book to be misleading. If you only work on one book at a time, the process will take about eight weeks. But this book is about the process I use. I make sure to stagger the books that I am working on, working on three or four books at a time. The books are in different stages of production: beginning, middle, and end. This helps ensure that I keep up with the production process so that I can release a book per month.

Publishing Your Book

A. Sending Files to Publisher—Time Frame of One Week

Sending the files to the publisher only takes about ten minutes. My publisher helps people self-publish books.

You can self-publish books on Create Space, which is part of Amazon, and their system works nicely. I know many self-published authors who use Create Space, so that might be a good option for you. You can certainly use my publisher and say that I recommended you. He will give you the same deal that he gives me.

When I send the book to my publisher, I fill out a form with the title of the book, the subtitle of the book, the author's name and any cowriters. I also send the book synopsis, which is the back-cover text of the book, with an author bio. He provides the ISBN for both the paperback and the e-book.

You need to fill out the form and then upload your Kindle cover. By now, your graphic designer should have returned the cover to you. You send your Kindle cover to him and then send your final manuscript after editing and proofreading is done. This process only takes about ten minutes, but I listed that it takes one day.

I have a strong relationship with my publisher, so he gives me priority service. It takes a week to get those files back from him, so he sends me a digital file to upload to Kindle. Then you log into Kindle and upload your Kindle file. Kindle takes about eight hours to make your book live on Amazon.

B. Ordering Your Paperback

When Bill, my publisher, sends the Kindle file back to me, he will also send the PDF of the paperback so that you can review it.

Make sure that you carefully proofread it and that there are no mistakes in it. You can then see the total page count in the PDF. Send your graphic designer the page count so that he or she can create a spine with the right dimensions for your book.

The spine of the book will vary in size, depending on the page count. The graphic designer needs your page count to create the spine. Once Bill sends you the PDF (usually the same day), you can message your graphic designer the page count and order your paperback cover. Your graphic designer will probably take a day or two to send you the file for the paperback cover. Then send the paperback cover to Bill so that he can publish the book.

If you're releasing the book through Create Space, you will follow a similar process. You will either create the PDF yourself or have it designed by Create Space. Create Space will send you a free copy of the PDF to review.

Look over the PDF to be sure it looks right. Get the page count from the PDF and send that to your graphic designer.

The graphic designer must create two covers: one for the paperback and one for the e-book. If Create Space is creating a cover, then they will handle that too. You want to make sure that you have extraordinary cover designs from a gifted cover designer. I've seen books designed by Create Space, but the covers weren't up to my standards.

C. Paperback Published in One Week

Since Bill and I have a close working relationship, he takes about a week to make the paperback live on Amazon. You can be assured that he will take good care of you. All the details of your book will pass on to Amazon. You will be able to see your paperback and your Kindle book live on Amazon in a week.

If everything goes right, your Kindle book and your paperback will appear together on Amazon in a search for your book title. But sometimes they might appear as two separate listings on two different pages. If that happens, contact Kindle and ask them to link the two editions of your book.

If someone finds your Kindle book, the same page should have a link to your paperback book. Many authors don't know about this. People might want to order the paperback edition of the book, but they can't find the correct page to do so. On the other hand, they might want to order the Kindle book, but they can only find the paperback. You want to contact Kindle within a few days to correct the mistakes if the books are not linked.

If you're publishing through Create Space, they will create and publish your paperback first. You can then have Create Space design your Kindle file and Kindle book.

Create Space will then publish the Kindle book a week or so later. Create Space can be very expensive, and I find that using Bill for my books is more cost-effective with a better streamlined process. Bill goes through the process quickly for me because I have published about thirty books with him. We have a great working relationship.

Important Points

A. Know your subject thoroughly so that you don't have to research it.

One way to record a book over a couple of days in twenty to thirty files is that you intimately know your subject matter. It takes quite a bit of experience to be able to sit down with a computer or recorder and record a book. Some people type a book on their laptop or desktop instead and have time to think. They write, rewrite, and edit as they go.

When you're recording, you have just one chance to record the book. Of course, you can edit it later, but it takes a lot more time to edit a recording. It makes sense for you to write a book about something that you know thoroughly and that you have extensive information about. That's why I can record and produce this book because I've written about twenty-five books in the last two years and fourteen books in the last twelve months.

I'm very experienced at writing an average of a book a month. I have my process down pat, so I know this subject very well. Like I've said, other people might teach you how to write a book in sixty days. But their books might be cheap and not well researched or of the best quality. They're just in the business of pumping out books. That is not my purpose. I write books with intentionality and meaning. I want all of my readers to learn and to be encouraged and personally developed as Christians.

My books are on topics that interest me with the right information. I have thoroughly researched them through the life I have lived and through my experience in the matter. My research is my life. I don't spend time reading and researching the material in any of my books. But I spend a lot of time reading and watching videos and researching the Christian faith in my personal life. As I gain information and grow as a Christian, I become more productive and more grounded. I have a lot to offer and a lot to share. I have learned about a subject, and then years later, I produce a book on what I have learned.

B. Have the mental capacity to record for three or four hours in two days.

I was talking to a friend yesterday about recording this book. He told me that the average person doesn't have the presence, the ability, or the strength of God to be able to produce a book as quickly as I can. You do need the mental capacity to be able to sit down and record twenty to thirty chapters over the course of two days. The process seems pretty simple to me because it's just a matter of organizing what you're going to say, drafting the chapter titles, and then writing bullet points. You will then sit down and record the material, just as if you were talking to someone face to face over coffee. I sit down and record with my computer on my lap.

I find that I'm really relaxed with a great capacity to be able to sit for hours and record a book. If you can't sit and record material for two hours, it might take you a lot longer to write a book than what I've described.

C. Develop a great relationship with your contractors: your editor, proofreader, designer, and publisher.

The reason that my publisher produces my books so quickly is because I'm his number one writer. We have an excellent relationship, and the price that he charges me to produce my books is minimal. He puts a priority on my work and drops everything when one of my books comes in to make sure that it's done as soon as possible. He takes longer to publish books from other people who use his services. I have built a strong relationship with my publisher over the course of thirty books, so we have a great relationship.

My editor and I also have an amazing working relationship. We have worked on at least twenty-two books together. We are great friends and talk outside of editing—on Facebook, following each other's pages and commenting on each other's posts.

I have an excellent relationship with my proofreader, and I speak to her two or three times a week on the phone. We have a wonderful friendship. She suggested that she proofread for me. She found some errors in my books, so we talked it over with Lisa. We arranged for her to become my proofreader.

I also have a great relationship with my cover designer, who has designed over thirty of my book covers. He puts a priority on my books as well. When you find him on Fiverr, his business information says that it takes eight days to get the cover design. But with me, he only takes two or three days, so he puts a rush on my work.

In order to be able to produce a book per month, you need to have other relationships in place. I have developed these over time. Since I have been working with all of these people for a while as a professional book writer and a professional author, I have built strong relationships with my team.

D. Work on different stages of several books at the same time, such as self-editing, Kindle cover design, book recording, and more.

I work on several books that are in different stages at the same time. For example, a Kindle cover might be in the process of design while Lisa is doing the first round of copy edits. Even though I am waiting a week for my cover to come back, I am also waiting a week for Lisa to finish the first round of edits before we do the read through.

During that week, my cover is being designed; Lisa is doing the first round of edits, and I am working on the first or second round of edits for the next book that I will send to Lisa. I'm always working on some aspect of a book: start, middle, or end. You can produce a book each month by working on three or four books at once.

The contact information for my editor, my publisher, my cover designer, and my proofreader follows.

Resources

A. My Publisher: Bill Vincent of Revival Waves of Glory Books & Publishing

I found out about Bill a few years ago when I was reading a book that he'd written. I looked up the publisher of the book, and he had published it himself. I wrote to him and found out that he was willing to publish my books too. We worked out a great deal, and I started to publish books through his company. Through the course of doing over thirty books with Bill, I became a great friend to him, and we have built a solid friendship.

Bill will include the following in a special package of $299 for you: an e-book, a paperback book, a hardcover book, and an audio book. (Note: Prices subject to change without notice.)

You can have all four of these things done: your Kindle file designed, your paperback produced, your hardcover book produced, and your audio book produced. You can order a book through me for $299 (price subject to change without notice) and have him create those four things. The price is much higher on Create Space. If you publish through Bill, you will need independent editing and a separate cover design. My covers cost me $200 each.

Bill is a hard worker and publishes mostly Christian books. He likes to read the books first before he accepts them or publishes them. He's a very studious person and is an author himself with over sixty books. He's written some wonderful books. He's a strong writer and a knowledgeable Christian. He started his business of self-publishing books simply to make things easier for himself. He eventually branched out into publishing books for other people. I happily recommend him to you as a publisher. If you are interested in his services, I suggest that you contact me. We can arrange to approach Bill together.

Bill's personal email is bill.vincent@yahoo.com
My email is survivors.sanctuary@gmail.com

B. My editor: Lisa Thompson

Lisa is a Christian, and she can competently edit both Christian and secular content. She can also edit fiction and nonfiction. She's very experienced and makes her living as an editor.

Many people write a book and think that a friend who is good at English can edit it for them. They might have another friend who offered to proofread it. They choose to use these people instead of using a professional because it costs less. Editing a book is a complex process that takes a unique skill set. Traditional publishing houses use developmental editors, copy editors, and proofreaders with as many as five sets of eyes on each book.

They work hard to find nearly every single error. The final proofreader at a traditional publishing house will still find mistakes that four other editors and proofreaders missed. As a writer, especially if you are self-published, you will want to present your work as professionally as possible.

You can approach Lisa yourself and tell her that you read about her services in this book. She'll treat you with respect and with love. She'll do a professional editing job on your book.

You can find out more about Lisa Thompson at www.writebylisa.com and email her at writebylisa@gmail.com for your editing needs.

C. My proofreader: Nicola

Nicola is a close friend of mine who is also a Christian. She works closely with Lisa, so if Lisa edits your book, Nicola might proofread it for you. You can also contact Nicola directly. You might have a book that's been professionally edited, and you want someone to proofread it. If so, contact Nicola, and she'll be happy to proofread your book.

Nicola has a great relationship with God. She's a strong Christian, open-minded and loving. You will enjoy working with her. She is also writing her own book as well, so she's an author too. She understands that your book is important to you, and she'll do the best work possible on your manuscript.

You can contact her at her email: nicolawhitehall777@gmail.com

D. My graphic designer: Akira007 on Fiverr.com

Akira007 is my graphic designer. He does a wonderful job on my book covers.

I suggest that you go to my Amazon Author Page to see my book covers. Look at the book covers that have been produced in the last two years to see if you like the quality and the style. My graphic designer, Akira007, did them for me. He has done a great job of producing them. I'm very happy with him and with his work. It would be really hard for me to switch designers. You will notice that a lot of them have brackets around the heading and about fifteen of them have very similar styles, so in a way, he's branded my books and done a tremendous job.

E. Create Space

You can contact Create Space here.

Visit Create Space and read all of the services that they offer. Create Space is very professional and will provide a quick turnaround on your books. They will provide you with a PDF, a paperback design, your Kindle book design, and your cover design. Look into them if you don't use Bill's services.

Closing Thoughts

This is a handy book on how to write a book, keys to writing a successful book, and how to maximize your book-writing efforts.

As I've said before, the key to writing one book per month is to have the ability and the focus to work on three to four books at a time. I also need to add that most of my books are thirty-five thousand words or less, which helps the process go quickly. Of course, if you have a full-time job, this might be hard for you to do. I receive a disability pension from the government, so I don't need to do any other work and can focus on writing books and other ministry-related activities.

I have a ministry of giving prophecies, and people donate to my ministry. I have a book-writing ministry. People donate money to finance my books.

I have free time to be able to write full-time, and that's what I do. You might be able to write a book in a month or in six weeks. It's possible. I've proven that it's possible to write fourteen books in twelve months. Once again, I'll emphasize that my books are quality books, and I'm proud of each one. I wouldn't allow any of my books to be published if I weren't happy with them. I'm happy with the content in this book.

I hope that you've been encouraged by this book. Of course, the book was ninety-nine cents. I'm sure that you got your money's worth out of it. I encourage you to read books about writing if you don't have the confidence to write your book. But once again, this is the process I use when I write a book.

For example, when I talk about marketing a book, I'm the first to confess that I haven't used Facebook ads or Amazon ads to promote my books. It doesn't make sense for me to use these ads as it costs more than a dollar per click to advertise each book, and my books only cost ninety-nine cents.

Every writer will have their own style, which they should use. I do some things differently and uniquely. I've described my process, and my books are successful. As such, I consider myself a successful writer. But I need to make something perfectly clear. I write books as a ministry and consider myself a preacher in my books rather than preaching in churches. In this way, I preach to twelve hundred to fourteen hundred readers every month.

I consider it a real honor to hear from readers as they share how their faith has exploded, and they've gone to another level. They've learned so much through my books. My books are exciting to them, and they enjoy reading them.

I've had a few people write to me and say that they ordered and read every one of my books, and they're very happy with me. Some of the people who read my books write reviews as well. It's always encouraging as a writer to read positive reviews for your books from people that you don't know. They haven't contacted you but have simply written a kind review of your book.

It's heartwarming to not only produce a quality book that I'm proud of but to have people write reviews, encourage me, and tell me how helpful my book was to them.

I pray that God will move you. I pray that God will give you inspiration and give you a great idea for a book and that his presence and his peace will be with you as you work together to write your book. Of course, this book talks about how to write a book, but I record most of my books. This speeds up the process and helps me write a book per month.

Other people might sit down, type out their books, and write a book per month, but I don't do that. I have some books that I type, such as my series on *Conversations with God*. But I don't write many books by typing them. I hope you've been encouraged to write your own book by what I've said here. I hope to hear from you when you decide to write, edit, or publish your own book.

Take the liberty to use my resources and write to me about your experience.

I'd love to hear from you

One of the ways that you can bless me as a writer is by writing an honest and candid review of my book on Amazon. I always read the reviews of my books, and I would love to hear what you have to say about this one.

Before I buy a book, I read the reviews first. You can make an informed decision about a book when you have read enough honest reviews from readers. One way to help me sell this book and to give me positive feedback is by writing a review for me. It doesn't cost you a thing but helps me and the future readers of this book enormously.

To read my blog, request a life-coaching session, request your own personal prophecy, request a visit to heaven, or to receive a personal message from your angel, you can also visit my website at http://personal-prophecy-today.com All of the funds raised through my ministry website will go toward the books that I write and self-publish.

To write to me about this book or to share any other thoughts, please feel free to contact me at my personal email address at survivors.sanctuary@gmail.com

You can also friend request me on Facebook at Matthew Robert Payne. Please send me a message if we have no friends in common as a lot of scammers now send me friend requests.

You can also do me a huge favor and share this book on Facebook as a recommended book to read. This will help me and other readers.

How to Sponsor a Book Project

If you have been blessed by this book, perhaps you might consider sponsoring a book for me. It normally costs me between $1,500 and $2,000 or more to produce each book that I write, depending on the length of the book.

If you seek the Holy Spirit about financing a book for me, I know that the Lord would be eternally grateful to you. Consider how much this book has blessed you and then think of hundreds or even thousands of people who would be blessed by a book of mine. As you are probably aware, the vast majority of my books are ninety-nine cents on Kindle, which proves to you that book writing is indeed a ministry for me and not a money-making venture. I would be very happy if you supported me in this.

If you have any questions for me or if you want to know what projects I am currently working on that your money might finance, you can write to me at survivors.sanctuary@gmail.com and ask me for more information. I would be pleased to give you more details about my projects.

You can sow any amount to my ministry by simply sending me money via the PayPal link at this address: http://personal-prophecy-today.com/support-my-ministry/

You can be sure that your support, no matter the amount, will be used for the publishing of helpful Christian books for people to read.

Other Books by Matthew Robert Payne

The Prophetic Supernatural Experience

Prophetic Evangelism Made Simple

Your Identity in Christ

His Redeeming Love: A Memoir

Writing and Self-Publishing Christian Nonfiction

Coping with your Pain and Suffering

Living for Eternity

Jesus Speaking Today

Great Cloud of Witnesses Speak

My Radical Encounters with Angels

Finding Intimacy with Jesus Made Simple

My Radical Encounters with Angels: Book Two

A Beginner's Guide to the Prophetic

Michael Jackson Speaks from Heaven

7 Keys to Intimacy with Jesus

Conversations with God: Book 1

Optimistic Visions of Revelation

Conversations with God: Book 2

Finding Your Purpose in Christ

Influencing your World for Christ: Practical Everyday Evangelism

Deep Calls unto Deep: Answering Questions on the Prophetic

My Visits to the Galactic Council of Heaven

The Parables of Jesus Made Simple:
Updated and Expanded Edition

Great Cloud of Witnesses Speak: Old and New

Walking under an Open Heaven

A Message from My Angel: Book 1

Interviews with the Two Witnesses: Enoch and Elijah Speak

Gaining Freedom from Sex Addictions: Breaking Free of
Pornography and Prostitutes

Mary Magdalene Speaks from Heaven: A Divine Revelation

Princess Diana Speaks from Heaven: A Divine Revelation

How to Hear God's Voice:
Keys to Conversational Two-Way Prayer

Apostle John Speaks from Heaven: A Divine Revelation

What I Believe

Great Cloud of Witnesses Speak: God's Generals

Apostle Peter Speaks from Heaven: A Divine Revelation

You can find my published books on my Amazon Author Page here: http://tinyurl.com/jq3h893

Upcoming Books:

19 Scriptures that Will Change Your Life

Apostle Paul Speaks from Heaven: A Divine Revelation

About Matthew Robert Payne

Matthew was raised in a Baptist church and was led to the Lord at the tender age of eight. He has experienced some pain and darkness in his life, which has given him a deep compassion and love for all people.

Today, he's a founding member and admin of a Facebook group called "Prophetic Training Group," and he invites you to join him there. Matthew has a commission from the Lord to train up prophets and to mentor others in the Christian faith. He does this through his Facebook posts and by writing relevant books on the Christian faith.

God has commissioned him to write at least fifty books in his life, and he spends his days writing and earning the money to self-publish. You can support him by donating money at http://personal-prophecy-today.com or by requesting any of the other services available through his ministry website.

Recently, the Lord has put it on his heart to start his own publishing company for other people's books called Christian Book Publishing USA. It is Matthew's hope to help some people self-publish their books in the future.

It is Matthew's prayer that this book has blessed you, and he hopes it will lead you into a deeper and more intimate relationship with God.

www.ingramcontent.com/pod-product-compliance
Lightning Source LLC
Chambersburg PA
CBHW052118070526
44584CB00017B/2540